W9-BOA-740

MILITARY VEHICLES

IAN GRAHAM

Heinemann Library
Chicago, Illinois

© 2003 Heinemann Library
a division of Reed Elsevier, Inc.
Chicago, Illinois

Customer Service 888-454-2279
Visit our website at www.heinemanlibrary.com

Design by Jo Hinton-Malivoire and Tinstar Design Limited (www.tinstar.co.uk)
Illustrations by Geoff Ward
Originated by Dot Gradations Ltd
Printed and bound in Hong Kong, China by South China Printing

07 06 05 04
10 9 8 7 6 5 4 3 2

Library of Congress Cataloging-in-Publication Data
Graham, Ian, 1953-
  Military vehicles / Ian Graham.
      v. cm. -- (Designed for success)
Includes bibliographical references and index.
Contents: Military vehicles -- Designing for war -- Battle tanks -- Closer
look: Abrams M1A2 main battle tank: design -- Closer look: Abrams M1A2
main battle tank: construction -- Closer look: Abrams M1A2 main battle
tank: performance -- Engine power -- Transporters -- Light armor --
Long-range firepower -- Protecting the column -- Special vehicles.
  ISBN 1-40342-655-4 (Library Binding-hardcover)
  1. Armored vehicles, Military--United States--Juvenile literature. 2.
Tanks (Military science)--United States--Juvenile literature. 3.
Vehicles, Military--United States--Juvenile literature. [1. Armored
vehicles, Military. 2. Vehicles, Military. 3. Tanks (Military science)]
I. Title. II. Series.
  UG446.5 .G6824 2003
  623.7'4--dc21

                        2002009340

Acknowledgments
The author and publishers are grateful to the following for permission to reproduce copyright material: pp. 1, 8 TRH Pictures/General Dynamics ; pp. 3, 5 (top), 7 (bottom), 15 (top), 17 (bottom), 19 (bottom), 21 (top), 21 (bottom), 23 (top), 24 TRH Pictures; p. 4 Popperfoto/Michael Urban/Reuters; pp. 5 (middle and bottom) TRH Pictures/A. Landau ; p. 6 PA Photos/Andrew Parsons; p. 7 (top) TRH Pictures/Christopher F. Foss; pp. 9 (top), 13 (middle) TRH Pictures/US Army; pp. 9 (middle), 13 (bottom), 26 General Dynamics; p. 9 (bottom) Corbis/ MPL/Peter Russell; p. 11 Popperfoto/Jack Dabaghian/Reuters; p. 12 Popperfoto/Matko Biljak/Reuters; p. 13 (top) Defense Visual Information Center; p. 14 TRH Pictures/M. Ingram; p. 15 (bottom)TRH Pictures/M. Roberts; p. 16 MPL; p. 17 (top) Popperfoto/Charles Platiau/Reuters; pp. 18, 19 (top), 27 (bottom) TRH Pictures/E. Nevill; p. 20 Popperfoto/Nikola Solic/Reuters; p. 22 TRH Pictures/US Department of Defense; p. 23 (bottom) Unknown; p. 25 (top) Aviation Picture Library; p. 25 (bottom) EPA; p. 27 (top) TRH Pictures/GIAT Industries; p. 28 British Museum; p. 29 TRH Pictures/IWM.

Cover photograph reproduced with permission of MPL.

Our thanks to Mark J. Adamic for his comments in the preparation of this book.

Every effort has been made to contact copyright holders of any material reproduced in this book. Any omissions will be rectified in subsequent printings if notice is given to the publishers.

Some words are shown in bold, **like this.** You can find out what they mean by looking in the glossary.

CONTENTS

MILITARY VEHICLES

Success in wartime depends on having powerful fighting forces. It also depends on being able to move troops, weapons, and supplies to the right place at the right time. This is the vitally important job of military vehicles.

Military forces use a wide variety of vehicles. Tanks, **self-propelled guns,** and rocket launchers are formidable mobile weapons. Trucks move troops and supplies. **Armored personnel carriers** and **light tanks** protect troops while they are moving around. **Reconnaissance** vehicles probe the land ahead of troops and spy on enemy forces. Recovery vehicles help other vehicles that have gotten into difficulty. Each is designed to do its own special job.

LEOPARD ON THE PROWL

The German Leopard 2 is one of the most fearsome military vehicles, a **main battle tank (MBT).**

- The Leopard 2 is so solidly constructed and carries so much **armor** that it weighs an astonishing 69 tons. That is as much as 40 typical family cars weigh.
- If it ran on ordinary wheels, it would sink into the ground. Instead, it runs on **tracks** that spread its weight over a greater area.
- A vehicle of this enormous weight needs an extremely powerful engine. The Leopard 2 is powered by a 1,500-**horsepower** diesel engine.

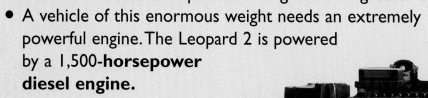

BORROWING FROM OTHER DESIGNS

Not every new military vehicle is designed from scratch. Time and money are saved by using parts that have already proved successful in other vehicles. The German Gepard anti-aircraft tank is built on the **chassis** of a Leopard MBT. **Radar** dishes on top of the **turret** search the sky for targets. The turret's twin guns are then trained on the approaching enemy aircraft.

TROOP TRANSPORT

The U.S. Bradley M2 Armored Fighting Vehicle (AFV) is designed to transport troops safely in the thick of the action in combat. Each vehicle carries a crew of three, and up to seven troops at up to 41 mph (66 km/hr). Its body is made from **aluminum,** a very lightweight metal, covered by light armor. Two guns are mounted on a rotating turret. They are used to give **covering fire** for troops entering and leaving the vehicle.

HEAVY MOVERS

Armies often need heavy construction and engineering vehicles. Some of these are also produced by modifying other vehicles. The U.S. M-728 Combat Engineer Vehicle is a military bulldozer. It is based on a M60A1 MBT.

Bradley M2 armored fighting vehicle

Crew: 3
Length: 21.3 ft (6.5 m)
Weight: 25.2 tons
Top speed: 41 mph (66 km/hr)
Armament: 25 mm gun
    antitank missile
    machine gun

BATTLE TANKS

Military vehicles are designed to work in some of the most difficult and dangerous conditions. The **main battle tank** (**MBT**) is one of the most important vehicles used in modern land warfare.

A tank designer has to strike a balance between firepower, crew protection, and mobility. Most tanks follow the same basic layout—an **armored hull** riding on twin **tracks** with a rotating gun **turret** on top. The tank has to be big enough for a crew of three or four to work inside. The commander is in overall control. A second member of the crew drives the tank. Two more, the gunner and loader, usually handle the main gun. Some tanks have an autoloader, a machine that replaces the loader. There also must be space to store the **shells** that the gun fires. The designer might choose to use a bigger gun or thicker **armor,** but these would make the tank heavier and less mobile. Thinner armor would be lighter but would offer less protection.

CHALLENGER 2

Britain's main battle tank, the Challenger 2, is armed with a **stabilized gun.** The gun is kept steady and pointed at its target even when the tank turns or drives over rough ground. Unusual for tanks today, the gun has a rifled **barrel.** That means grooves spiral down inside its length. When a shell is fired down the barrel, the grooves make it spin. A spinning shell is more stable in the air and therefore more accurate.

Challenger 2 MBT

Crew: 4
Length: 37.7 ft (11.5 m)
Weight: 70 tons
Top speed: 37 mph (59 km/hr)
Armament: 120 mm main gun,
      7.62 mm chain gun
      7.62 mm anti-aircraft gun

EXPLODING ARMOR

The Russian T-90 MBT is protected by one of the strangest types of armor used today. It's called Explosive Reactive Armor (ERA). It is actually designed to explode when an **artillery** shell hits it! By exploding, it stops the shell or antitank **round** from bursting through the tank's hull.

TANK WITHOUT TURRETS

The Swedish Stridsvagn Strv-103 has a very unusual design. It has no gun **turret**. This makes it very low and more difficult for enemy tanks to hit. Without a turret, the gun is fixed in position. It can't be raised or turned. To aim it, the tank is turned until it points in the right direction. Then the whole tank is tilted to raise the gun to the right angle. The disadvantage of this design is that the gun can't be fired while the tank is moving.

ABRAMS M1A2 MBT
DESIGNED TO SURVIVE

The M1A2 is the latest version of the high-tech M1 Abrams tank. Designers made the Abrams tank flatter and lower than most other tanks. This makes it more difficult for enemy fire to hit it. The sides of its **turret** slope in at an angle to deflect bullets and rockets. If an antitank **round** hits the top of the tank, panels there are designed to explode outward. This stops the round from bursting inside the tank. The M1A2's job is to attack the enemy head-on. Because it is most likely to be fired at from straight ahead, its designers put the thickest **armor** at the front. It is powered by a **gas turbine** engine (see pages 16–17).

LOW PROFILE

Designers wanted to keep the front of the Abrams M1A2 as low as possible. Therefore, the driver has to lie down on his or her back instead of sitting upright. The space is so cramped that there is no room for a steering wheel. Instead, the driver steers with a T-shaped bar, similar to motorcycle handlebars, between the knees. Twisting the right handgrip starts the tank moving. Turning the bar steers it. A pedal under the driver's right foot operates the brake.

The M1A2 Abrams is designed to be the best tank on any battlefield.

SIDESKIRTS

A tank's wheels and **tracks** are the weakest part in its design. The turret and **hull** are heavily armored, but the wheels and tracks are outside the armor and more easily damaged. If a tank's tracks or wheels become damaged, it cannot **maneuver** and it will soon be blown up by the enemy. The Abrams has armor-plated sideskirts attached over the top half of the tracks to give them some protection.

TAKING IN A VIEW

A tank crew needs to be able to see outside the tank. However, in combat, the crew is sealed inside. The solution to their problem is to use **periscopes.**

- The commander of an Abrams M1A2 has six periscopes so he or she can look out in any direction.
- The driver has another three periscopes.
- The gunner has a viewfinder for looking at targets.

NIGHT SIGHT

The tank also has an infra-red imaging system for seeing in dark or smoky conditions. It detects the heat given off by hot objects such as vehicle engines. The hotter an object is, the brighter it looks. Vehicles or guns that have stopped stay hot for a while. They, too, can be detected by the infra-red system, even when they are hidden under **camouflage** netting or **foliage,** like the gun here.

ABRAMS M1A2 MBT

CONSTRUCTION

An Abrams M1A2 **main battle tank** (MBT) is built from more than 5,000 parts at a cost of more than $4 million. It has two main sections, the **hull** and the **turret.** The hull is cut from steel sheets up to 11.8 inches. (30 centimeters) thick and welded together. The turret is made separately, and then the two are fitted together.

Both the hull and the turret have to be made accurately. They have to fit together closely enough to keep gas and other harmful chemicals and particles out of the tank. Air sucked into the tank for the crew to breathe is cleaned by filters. These remove all harmful or **radioactive** substances. Once the engine and all the electronic systems are installed, the final job is to fit the **tracks.** Every Abrams M1A2 is then driven on a special test track and its main gun is test-fired. Engineers check that everything works properly on each tank before it is handed over to the army.

Rubber track pads

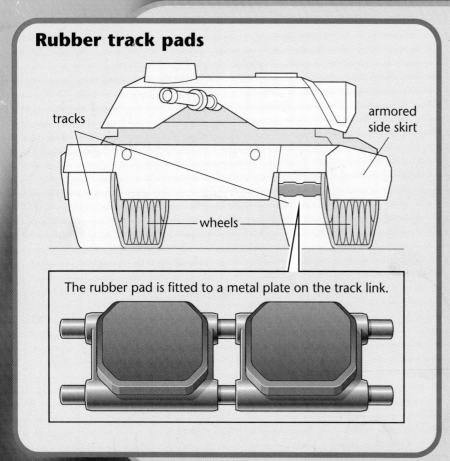

tracks

armored side skirt

wheels

The rubber pad is fitted to a metal plate on the track link.

TRACKS

Each of the Abrams tank tracks is 49.9 feet (15.2 meters) long and made from 79 metal links, like a flattened bicycle chain. The tank's weight rests on tough rubber pads fitted to the links. These pads can be replaced when they wear out, so the whole link does not have to be replaced. The pads also increase grip and reduce noise when the tank is driven on roads. However, the rubber pads cannot grip ice. Sometimes the tank has to operate on slippery surfaces. Then, the rubber pads on every fifth link are replaced by metal plates, called cleats, which can bite into the surface better.

ARMOR

The design of a tank's **armor** is a closely guarded secret. The Abrams tank has armor made from **depleted uranium** encased in steel. Depleted uranium is a waste product of the **nuclear** industry. It a very dense, or tightly packed, metal. It stops dart-shaped antitank **rounds,** also made of depleted uranium, from punching holes in the tank. The uranium is slightly radioactive. But, because it is encased in steel, the radiation level inside the tank is lower than the natural radiation outside.

Abrams M1A2 MBT

Crew: 4
Length: 32.2 ft (9.8 m)
Weight: 77.8 tons
Top speed: 42 mph (67 km/hr)
Armament: 120 mm main gun
7.62 mm machine gun
7.62 mm anti-aircraft gun
12.7 mm anti-aircraft gun

ABRAMS M1A2 MBT

FAST AND FURIOUS

The M1A2 is surprisingly swift for such a heavy vehicle. So what happens if an Abrams tank driver opens the **throttle** and takes off as fast as possible? In less than six seconds, the 78-ton vehicle is going more than 19 mph (30 km/hr). A few seconds later, it can be going 42 mph (67 km/hr). If it has to stop, its brakes are amazingly powerful. Under full braking, the tank can stop from 31 mph (50 km/hr) in about 9.8 feet (3 meters). Its firepower is impressive, too. Its massive 120-mm gun can destroy six different targets up to 2.5 miles (4 kilometers) away within a minute.

FIRE CONTROL

When an Abrams tank's crew spots a target, the following occurs:

- A **laser range finder** fires an intense beam of light at it.
- The time it takes for the reflection to bounce back is measured, and the tank's fire-control computer uses this time to calculate exactly how far away the target is.
- The computer calculates the gun's direction and elevation, or how high it must be raised. It allows for wind speed, wind direction, and even the slightest bend in the gun **barrel.**

Within a few seconds of spotting a target, the gun is locked onto it and ready to fire.

KEEPING COOL

With all the hatches closed, the temperature inside a tank's cramped crew compartment soon soars. The Abrams M1A2 is therefore equipped with a cooling system. This keeps the air temperature below 95°F (35°C) and surfaces that the crew has to touch below 126°F (52°C).

ABRAMS IN ACTION

During the 1991 Gulf War to liberate Kuwait from an Iraqi invasion, a tank force including 2,000 U.S. Abrams tanks destroyed nearly 2,000 Iraqi tanks. Not a single Abrams tank was lost. The Abrams tanks could open fire when they were still about 3,300 feet (1,000 meters) beyond the range of Iraq's Soviet-made tanks.

In this picture, the damage done to an Iraqi tank by a U.S. **shell** is clearly visible.

SMOOTH RIDE

The Abrams tank runs on seven wheels, but none of them are driven by the engine. The engine drives a pair of toothed wheels called drive sprockets at the back of the tank. The teeth fit holes in the **tracks** and drive them around. The seven road wheels support the weight of the tank. Each wheel is attached to a rod called a **torsion** bar that twists when the wheel is pushed up by a bump. The torsion bars act like springs. They keep the tracks pressed down on bumpy, uneven ground while the tank glides along smoothly.

DESIGNING FOR WAR

Military vehicles are designed according to the jobs they have to do. As you have seen, **main battle tanks (MBTs),** the biggest tanks on a battlefield, are very heavy because of their massive **armor.** However, **armored personnel carriers** and **light tanks** are made small and **maneuverable.** This means they can move around nimbly and quickly to avoid attack by heavy weapons.

Designers have to think about many other things, too. How are their vehicles going to be transported? Are they light enough to be lifted by helicopter? Will they fit inside a transport plane? Can they travel on public roads under their own power, or will they need to be towed on trailers? The cost of producing each vehicle is also an important factor.

GOING TO WAR

Military vehicles often have to travel long distances. Designers have to be sure that their vehicles can be carried by other transport vehicles. The British Stormer 30 light tank can be airlifted by a Sikorsky CH-53 helicopter or inside a Lockheed C-130 transport plane. It can also be carried by truck and by train. It can even land at sea using **amphibious** landing craft.

Stormer 30 light tank

Crew: 3

Length: 17.2 ft (5.3 m)

Weight: 14.5 tons

Top speed: 50 mph (80 km/hr)

Armament: 30 mm cannon

      2 machine guns

      2 grenade launchers

      optional missile launcher

CREW SAFETY

Designing a vehicle to give its crew maximum protection is not simply a matter of surrounding the crew with thick armor. Some antitank weapons work by making chunks of metal, called spall, fly off the inside of the vehicle. Spall flying around inside a vehicle is deadly. The passenger compartment of the U.S. M113 armored personnel carrier is lined with a supertough material called Kevlar to prevent spall.

CAMOUFLAGE

Most military vehicles are painted in colors that help them blend in with their surroundings. Browns and greens are used to match soil and green plants. Lighter sandy browns are used in desert regions. This technique is called **camouflage.** Camouflage not only matches a vehicle's color to its surroundings, it also breaks up the vehicle's shape and outline so that it is harder to identify. Netting and **foliage** are used to further break up a vehicle's shape and hide it from aircraft and ground forces.

ENGINE POWER

A military vehicle's engine is designed to do everything a car engine does, but it also has to deal with specialized problems of military service. These engines are designed to provide the most power in the smallest space. Military engines also have to be able to run nonstop all day without overheating, even when the vehicle is not moving. They have to be quick and easy to repair or to take out and replace.

Almost all large military land vehicles are powered by **diesel engines** because of their strength and reliability. A few military land vehicles use **gas turbines** similar to fighter-plane **jet engines.** Gas turbines pack even more power into a smaller space and need less maintenance to keep them going. They have two disadvantages, however. They burn a lot of fuel, and they produce very hot **exhaust** gases that **heat-seeking missiles** can detect.

ENGINE POSITION

Most tanks have their engines at the back, but the designers of the Israeli Merkava tank put its engine at the front. One advantage of this design is that the engine gives the crew extra protection, similar to very thick **armor.** It also enabled the designers to put a door in the back of the tank, where the engine would normally be. In fighting conditions, the crew can enter and leave the tank more safely through the back, instead of the usual way through hatches on top.

JET POWER

The French Leclerc **main battle tank (MBT)** is one of the few military land vehicles with a gas turbine engine. It uses it differently from the Abrams tank. Most of the time the Leclerc tank is powered by a 1,500-**horsepower** diesel engine. However, when it stops, the diesel engine is shut down and a small gas turbine supplies the tank with electrical power. This means that the main engine does not need to be kept running when the tank is standing still.

Leclerc MBT

Crew: 3
Length: 32.5 ft (9.9 m)
Weight: 54.5 tons
Top speed: 44 mph (71 kph)
Armament: 120 mm main gun
      12.7-mm machine gun
      7.62-mm anti-aircraft gun

This is the engine that powers the U.S. M1 Abrams MBT.

FUEL

Most engines are designed to burn only one type of fuel. Using a different fuel can damage the engine. Some military engines are designed to be able to burn several different fuels so that they can use whatever is available. The U.S. M1 Abrams and Russian T-90 tanks have multifuel engines that can burn a variety of fuels, including diesel oil, gasoline, and jet aircraft fuel.

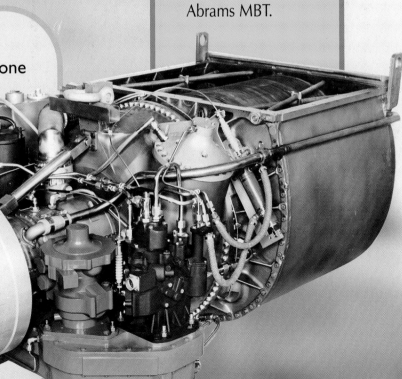

TRANSPORTERS

When an army goes to war, thousands of troops and thousands of tons of supplies have to be moved into position. An army's transport vehicles are as important as its weapons.

Military transport vehicles range from small troop carriers such as jeeps, to huge trucks for moving heavy cargo. They have to be able to go anywhere, so they usually have **all-wheel drive.** The tires are deeply grooved to grip soft and loose surfaces. In some cases, the crew can even change the pressure of the air in the tires from inside the cab. Letting some air out of the tires allows them to squash down onto the ground so that they offer a better grip. The same vehicle can often be supplied with different bodies for carrying people, cargo, or weapons.

MULTIPURPOSE VEHICLE

The U.S. Army's High Mobility Multipurpose Wheeled Vehicle (HMMWV) is nicknamed the Humvee or Hummer. It is one of the most rugged and versatile light military vehicles in the world. It has **four-wheel drive** for maximum grip off-road and a high ground clearance for driving over rough ground. It can be transported by air and even dropped by parachute. Its designers have produced eleven different versions of the Humvee. These include general-purpose troop or cargo carriers, missile carriers, battlefield ambulances, and a version for towing **artillery** guns.

CARGO TRANSPORT

The M-939 truck is an army cargo transport truck. It can carry up to 5.6 tons of supplies on- or off-road up to 65 mph (105 km/hr). It can also tow trailers or other vehicles that weigh up to 10.6 tons. The basic truck can be supplied with six different bodies. It can also be fitted with a **winch** to pull itself, or another vehicle, out of trouble. By the late 1990s, the U.S. Army had more than 30,000 M-939s.

Oshkosh Heavy Expanded Mobility Tactical Truck

Crew: 2
Length: 33.5 ft (10.2 m)
Weight: 19.7 tons
Top speed: 57 mph (92 km/hr)

HEAVY HAULERS

The Oshkosh Heavy Expanded Mobility Tactical Truck (HEMTT) is designed to carry up to 11.1 tons of cargo wherever the U. S. Army's tanks go. Its job is to keep the tanks and their crews supplied with everything they need to keep moving and fighting. All of its eight wheels are driven by its **445-horsepower diesel engine.** It can even be driven through water up to 3.9 feet (1.2 meters) deep. More than 15,000 HEMTTs have been built since 1982.

LIGHT ARMOR

Troops are often sent to war-torn parts of the world to help keep the peace. If there is a strong likelihood of attack, they travel in **armored** fighting vehicles (AFVs). A typical AFV weighs 16 to 22 tons and has a rotating gun **turret** similar to a tank's. An AFV designer has to decide whether to mount the vehicle on wheels or tank **tracks.** A tracked vehicle can move around easily on ground where a wheeled vehicle would get stuck. However, a wheeled vehicle is faster than a tracked vehicle. Which to choose depends on how the vehicle will be used.

WARRIOR

The British Warrior armored vehicle has lightweight **aluminum** armor that protects its soldiers against **shrapnel**, **mines,** and even small armor-piercing **rounds.** If it needs more protection, extra armor plates can be added. It has enough room inside for a crew of three, plus up to seven soldiers. It can be used for **reconnaissance,** security patrols, rescue work, **artillery** command, and resupply duties. It can be equipped with a range of weapons, from machine guns to **mortars** and missiles.

Warrior AFV

Crew: 3 (+7 soldiers)

Length: 20. 7 ft (6.3 m)

Weight: 26.8 tons

Top speed: 47 mph (75 km/hr)

Armament: 30 mm cannon

7.62 mm machine gun

2 missile launchers

The French ERC 90 F1 Lynx armored vehicle is unusual. It can be equipped with special water jets designed to propel it through water at around 5 mph (7 km/hr).

WATER POWER

Some AFVs are light enough to float across rivers. Their **hulls** are specially designed to be watertight. However, their designers do not usually include any special equipment to propel them through water. They just use their tracks. Tracks are not designed for propulsion in water, but they catch the water just enough to keep a vehicle slowly moving.

FUTURE LIGHT ARMOR

The next generation of light-armor vehicles is now being designed. The European Multi-Role Armored Vehicle (MRAV) is a modular vehicle. This means it is made from a series of parts, or modules, which can be put together in different ways to create different versions of the vehicle. The base vehicle is an **eight-wheel-drive chassis.** A mission module is then mounted on this. The choice of module depends on the type of mission. One mission module can be replaced by another one in less than an hour.

During a battle, ground forces may have to attack targets tens or hundreds of miles away. **Self-propelled howitzers** and rocket launchers are designed to do exactly this.

Tanks attack targets that their crews can see, up to about 16,400 feet (5,000 meters) away. Howitzers can throw a **shell** up to 19 to 25 miles (30 to 40 kilometers) away. For targets even farther away, a different type of weapon is needed. Instead of blasting a shell out of a **barrel,** self-propelled launch vehicles fire rocket-propelled **warheads** up to several hundred miles. **Self-propelled guns** are designed to move into position quickly, fire their shells or rockets, and then move quickly away. Because these vehicles usually operate behind the front line, they do not need the heavy **armor** of a **main battle tank.** Being light, with little armor, makes them more **maneuverable.**

HOWITZERS

The U.S. M109A6 Paladin looks like a tank, but it is actually a self-propelled howitzer designed to hit targets up to 19 miles (30 kilometers) away.

- Its main weapon is a 155 mm cannon.
- Its 440-**horsepower diesel engine** can move the 29-ton **tracked** vehicle at up to 40 mph (64 km/hr).
- It can fire its first **round** within 60 seconds of coming to a halt.
- There is enough space inside the armored **hull** for a commander, driver, gunner, loader, and 39 rounds of ammunition.

MULTIPLE LAUNCH ROCKET SYSTEM

The U.S. Multiple Launch Rocket System (MLRS) is a tracked vehicle armed with twelve **surface-to-surface** rockets or missiles. The launching tubes are mounted on a modified Bradley M2 armored fighting vehicle **chassis.** The chassis had to be made longer to carry the rocket launcher. Target information is transmitted to the vehicle's computer, which aims the rockets and tells the crew when they are ready to be fired. The MLRS can fire rockets and missiles with ranges from 10 to 185 miles (15 to 300 kilometers).

ROCKETS ON WHEELS

HIMARS is an **artillery** rocket system being developed in the United States. It has the firepower of the MLRS, but it is on a wheeled chassis instead of tracks. It is about half the weight of the MLRS, so it can move faster. HIMARS can get into position, fire, and move on before its launch site can be attacked. HIMARS is designed to fit inside a C-130 transport plane. It is expected to enter service in 2005.

HIMARS High Mobility Artillery Rocket System

Crew: 3
Length: 23.0 ft (7.0 m)
Weight: 12.2 tons
Top speed: 53 mph (85 km/hr)

PROTECTING THE COLUMI

Military forces can be attacked from the air at any time. Vehicles have been specially designed to detect air attacks and fight them off.

Tanks and **armored** fighting vehicles (AFVs) travel with troops and supply **convoys** to protect them. Whenever possible, helicopters and fighters also give air cover. There are also specially designed air defense vehicles. **Radar** vehicles search the sky for incoming enemy aircraft. **Self-propelled** anti-aircraft guns and air-defense vehicles armed with missiles fight them off. Attacks also may come from ground forces, so ground and air **reconnaissance** vehicles keep a good lookout.

ANTI-AIRCRAFT GUNS
The Ukrainian ZSU-23-4 Shilka is a self-propelled anti-aircraft gun. It rides on a **chassis** with **tracks.** It has **stabilized guns,** so it can fire on the move. A radar dish mounted on the top detects and tracks targets on the ground and in the air. The targets may be stationary, such as missile launchers, or moving, such as aircraft in flight. Targets picked up by the radar are then attacked by four automatic cannons on the **turret.**

ZSU-23-4 Shilka anti-aircraft vehicle

Crew: 4

Length: 21.3 ft (6.5 m)

Weight: 23 tons

Top speed: 31 mph (50 km/hr)

Armament: Four 23-mm anti-aircraft g

AIR DEFENSE

The same weapon system can be mounted on different types of vehicles. The Roland air-defense missile system is designed to deal with low-flying enemy aircraft. It can be mounted on its own truck for maximum mobility or on a towed trailer. A radar dish on top locates targets up to 12 miles (20 kilometers) away. It tracks them until they come within the missiles' range of 4, 5, or 8 miles (6, 8, or 11 kilometers). Two missiles are carried ready to fire, with another eight stored inside.

PLANES WITHOUT PILOTS

Spying on enemy forces from aircraft is very dangerous because of the risk of being shot down. So, Unmanned Aerial Vehicles (UAVs) are increasingly being used. They are designed to circle over the enemy for hours or even days, sending pictures directly to commanders and frontline troops. There are two types of UAVs:

- Remotely Piloted Vehicles (RPVs), such as the U.S. Predator, are flown from the ground by a pilot who has a control panel.
- Newly developed UAVs, such as the U.S. Global Hawk, are more advanced. Once programmed with a mission, Global Hawk takes off, flies the mission, and lands itself automatically.

The U.S. Global Hawk unmanned spy plane flew its first military mission over Afghanistan in 2001.

SPECIAL VEHICLES

Military forces use many of the same vehicles used in the construction industry, including diggers, loaders, dump trucks, cranes, and bulldozers, plus some more specialized vehicles. These special-purpose vehicles include bridge layers and **armored** recovery vehicles. Bridge-laying vehicles put temporary bridges in place. The fastest of them can lay a bridge for troops and vehicles to cross within a few minutes. Some of these vehicles are built from converted tanks.

Some military transport work also requires specially designed vehicles. Recovery vehicles have to be able to go anywhere so that they can lift or pull other vehicles out of trouble. **Main battle tanks (MBTs),** on the other hand, can be driven on roads. However, they are so heavy that their **tracks** can badly damage road surfaces. For this reason, they are often transported on trailers.

LAYING BRIDGES

The Wolverine Heavy Assault Bridge System built on an Abrams M tank **chassis.**

- It can lay a bridge strong enough to carry a battle tank over a 79-foot (24-meter) gap in less t five minutes.
- The vehicle carries bridge in four sectio
- **Hydraulic** arms assemble the bridge and slide it out over the gap.

RECOVERY VEHICLES

Military vehicles can operate in very difficult conditions, but they do sometimes break down or get stuck in soft ground. When they do, recovery vehicles are sent to pull them out—if they are still worth rescuing. These vehicles are equipped with **winches** and sometimes a crane to lift or drag another vehicle. Some recovery vehicles are based on wheeled trucks. The biggest and heaviest are built on a tank chassis with tracks. Recovery vehicles based on tanks carry the thickest armor, so they can operate in more dangerous combat conditions.

A vehicle as heavy as a main battle tank (MBT) needs an equally powerful recovery vehicle to come to its aid.

Oshkosh M1070 Heavy Equipment Transporter

Crew: 2 (+ 4 passengers)
Length: 30.2 ft (9.2 m)
Weight: 20.7 tons
Top speed: depends on load

TRANSPORTING TANKS

The U.S. Oshkosh M1070 Heavy Equipment Transporter has the important job of moving the heaviest military loads. It can even carry Abrams battle tanks. The M1070 is an **eight-wheel-drive tractor unit** that pulls a trailer that carries the load. The whole rig can weigh up to 117 tons. Such an enormously heavy vehicle needs a very powerful engine to haul its load on level ground and up slopes. It is powered by a 500-**horsepower**, 12-liter, **turbocharged diesel engine.**

This table of information compares the basic specifications of some of today's military vehicles.

Vehicle	Country of origin	Length (ft/m)	Weight (tons)	Top speed (mph/ km/hr)	Main g... (mm)
Abrams M1A2 MBT	United States	32.3/9.8	77.8	42/67	120
Bradley M2 AFV	United States	21.3/6.5	25.2	41/66	25
Challenger 2 MBT	UK	37.7/11.5	70.0	37/59	120
HIMARS rocket system	United States	23.0/7.0	12.2	53/85	none
Leclerc MBT	France	32.5/9.9	61.0	44/71	120
Leopard 2 MBT	Germany	25.3/7.7	69.4	45/72	120
Merkava MBT	Israel	28.9/8.8	67.2	28/46	120
Oshkosh M977 HEMTT	United States	33.5/10.2	19.7	57/92	none
Oshkosh M1070 Transporter	United States	30.2/9.2	20.7	variable	none
Paladin M109A6 **howitzer**	United States	31.8/9.7	32.3	40/64	155
Stormer 30 **light tank**	UK	17.2/5.3	14.5	50/80	30
Strv-103 MBT	Sweden	29.5/9.0	47.6	31/50	105
T-90 MBT	Russia	31.2/9.5	52.1	40/65	125
Warrior **armored** vehicle	UK	20.7/6.3	26.9	47/75	30
ZSU-23-4 anti-aircraft vehicle	Ukraine	21.3/6.5	21.7	31/50	23 x 4

LEONARDO'S TANK

The great Italian artist, sculptor, engineer, and scientist, Leonardo da Vinci (1452–1519), made many drawings of machines that were far ahead of their time. Among them, there is a strange machine that looks like a huge metal pie plate. It rides on four wheels and cannons point out in all directions. It is a battle tank, designed more than 400 years before the first tank was actually built.

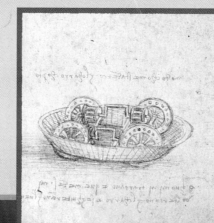

FURTHER READING

Bartlett, Richard. *Know It! U.S. Army Fighting Vehicles*. Chicago: Heinemann Library, 2003.

Black, Michael A. *Tanks: The M1A1 Abrams*. Danbury, Conn.: Scholastic Library Publishing, 2000.

Brown, Deni. *Look Inside Cross-Sections: Tanks*. New York: Dorling Kindersley Publishing, 1998.

Cornish, Geoff. *Tanks*. Minneapolis, Minn.: Lerner Publishing Group, 2003.

Green, Michael. *Main Battle Tanks*. Minnetonka, Minn.: Capstone Press, Inc., 2001.

THE FIRST TANK

The first practical tank was the British Mark I, built during the World War I. It was called a tank to keep its real purpose a secret. The Mark I weighed 31.9 tons. Its top speed was only 2.8 mph (4.5 km/hr). Its guns were mounted in its sides. The Mark I was used for the first time on September 15, 1916, at the Battle of the Somme.

GLOSSARY

all-wheel drive method of increasing a vehicle's grip on the ground by powering all of its wheels

aluminum lightweight metal used in vehicle construction

amphibious designed to be used on land and in water

armor thick plates of metal or other materials that protect military vehicles

armored personnel carrier vehicle, protected by armor, used to carry troops safely under fire

artillery large caliber guns or cannons that fire shells over long distances

barrel long tube through which a gun fires its bullets or artillery shells

camouflage method for making a vehicle more difficult to see or identify. Colored paint or netting is used to make it blend into its surroundings.

chassis main frame of a military vehicle that the rest of the vehicle is built on

convoy group of vehicles traveling together

covering fire shooting at enemy troops to stop them from attacking friendly troops while they are entering or leaving vehicles or moving around in the open

depleted uranium type of heavy, tightly packed metal left over when fuel for nuclear power plants or atomic bombs is made

diesel engine type of engine that burns a fuel called diesel oil. Diesel engines are used by many military vehicles because they are tough and reliable.

eight-wheel-drive describes a system that connects a vehicle's engine to all eight of its wheels

exhaust hot gases given out by an engine

four-wheel drive system that connects a vehicle's engine to all four of its wheels

foliage a plant's leaves

gas turbine type of engine used to power some military vehicles

heat-seeking missile weapon that hits a target by detecting the heat it gives out and flying toward it

horsepower ability to to do work that is roughly equal to the work that one horse can do, or about 746 watts of electrical power

howitzer artillery weapon that can raise its short or medium length barrel to a steep angle

hull main body of a large or heavy vehicle

hydraulic operated by the pressure of a liquid forced through pipes

jet engine type of engine used by some military vehicles

laser device that produces an intense beam of light

light tank lightly armed and armored vehicle, often used for reconnaissance

main battle tank (MBT) biggest and most powerful of an army's tanks

maneuver move or steer in a planned way

mine explosive device laid on, or under, the ground so that it explodes when a vehicle drives over it or someone steps on it

mortar small cannon with a short barrel

nuclear having to do with nuclei, the particles at the center of atoms. Nuclear weapons use energy released from atomic nuclei.

periscope device that uses mirrors or prisms (triangular blocks of glass) to let someone see something that is not in the direct line of sight

radar shortened term for Radio Detection and Ranging, a method of finding distant objects by sending out radio waves and picking up reflections that bounce back

radioactive having or giving out radiation

range finder device for finding out how far away an object is

reconnaissance obtaining information about an enemy's activities

round single bullet, artillery shell, or tank shell

self-propelled gun gun that has its own engine and so does not need to be towed by another vehicle

shell hollow metal case filled with an explosive and fired from a gun

shrapnel shell fragments; pieces of metal that fly out from an exploding shell

stabilized gun gun that keeps its barrel pointing at a target even if the tank carrying the gun is turning or driving over rough ground

surface-to-surface type of missile that is fired from a vehicle on the ground at targets that are also on the ground

throttle the part of an engine that varies the amount of fuel or air, or both, that flow into the engine. When a vehicle's driver presses the accelerator pedal, the throttle opens and the engine speeds up.

torsion twisting

tracks flexible metal bands made from a series of links, like bicycle chains, that are fitted to some military vehicles, especially tanks. Tracks enable a vehicle to be driven over soft ground without slipping or sinking.

tractor unit part of an articulated truck that contains the engine and pulls the trailer

turbocharged boosted in power by a turbocharger. A turbocharger forces extra air into an engine to burn more fuel and produce more power.

turret revolving armored structure on a vehicle that protects one or more guns mounted within it

warhead explosive part of a missile

winch drum driven by an engine or electric motor. As the drum rotates, it pulls in a cable or rope that is wound around the drum.

INDEX